Helen Paiba was one of the most committed, knowledgeable and acclaimed children's booksellers in Britain. For more than twenty years she owned and ran the Children's Bookshop in Muswell Hill, London, which under her guidance gained a superb reputation for its range of children's books and for the advice available to its customers.

Helen was also involved with the Booksellers Association for many years and served on both its Children's Bookselling Group and the Trade Practices Committee.

In 1995 she was given honorary life membership of the Booksellers Association of Great Britain and Ireland in recognition of her outstanding services to the association and to the book trade. In the same year the Children's Book Circle (sponsored by Books for Children) honoured her with the Eleanor Farjeon Award, given for distinguished service to the world of children's books.

Books in this series

Animal Stories for 5 Year Olds

Animal Stories for 6 Year Olds

Funny Stories for 5 Year Olds

Funny Stories for 6 Year Olds

Funny Stories for 7 Year Olds

Funny Stories for 8 Year Olds

Magical Stories for 5 Year Olds

Magical Stories for 6 Year Olds

Scary Stories for 7 Year Olds

Animal stories

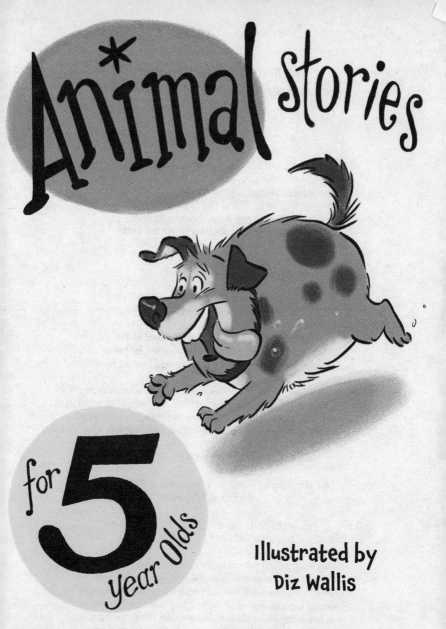

for 5 year olds

Illustrated by
Diz Wallis

Chosen by Helen Paiba

MACMILLAN CHILDREN'S BOOKS

In memory of John Smith,
an inspiration to children's booksellers

First published 2000 by Macmillan Children's Books

This edition published 2017 by Macmillan Children's Books
an imprint of Pan Macmillan
20 New Wharf Road, London N1 9RR
Associated companies throughout the world
www.panmacmillan.com

ISBN 978-1-5098-3877-6

1 3 5 7 9 8 6 4 2

A CIP catalogue record for this book is available from
the British Library.

Typeset by SX Composing DTP, Rayleigh, Essex
Printed and bound by CPI Group (UK) Ltd, Croydon CR0 4YY

Contents

When You Are Six

Sheila Lavelle

Emma had ten goldfish, seven rabbits, five hamsters, two tortoises, and a parrot that could sing *God Save the Queen*.

But Emma wanted a dog.

"Please, Mum," she said one morning at breakfast-time. "I would look after it. I would feed it and brush it and take it for walks, all by myself."

"No, Emma," said Mum, pouring

cornflakes into a bowl. "You're only five years old. You're much too little to have a dog."

"Couldn't I just have a little dog?" said Emma.

Dad looked at Emma over the top of his newspaper.

"Stop pestering, Emma," he said. "You're too young to have a dog. I don't want to hear any more about it."

Emma poured milk over her cornflakes.

"When will I be old enough?" she asked.

"When you are six," said Mum.

Emma counted on her fingers. This was March, and her birthday

2

was in June. That was three whole
months from now. It seemed a long
time to wait.

Then Emma had an idea. She ran
upstairs and brought down a toy
dog with pink ears and a curly
tail.

"Look, Mum. Here's Muffin," she
said. "He's a pretend dog. I can
practise feeding him and brushing
him and taking him for walks.
Then when I get my real dog, I'll
know how to look after it."

"That's very sensible of you,
Emma," said Dad. He swallowed
the last of his toast and
marmalade and went out to dig the
garden.

After breakfast, Mum and Emma and Muffin went to the library. While Mum was choosing her books, Emma looked on the shelf marked ANIMALS. She could read the word ANIMALS because she had an animal book at home.

She found books about elephants and chimpanzees, crocodiles and snakes, bears and kangaroos. But there was nothing about dogs, so she asked the librarian.

"You're looking in the wrong place," said the librarian. She showed Emma another shelf marked PETS.

Emma thought it was silly to have PETS and ANIMALS on

different shelves. Pets were animals, weren't they? But she didn't bother to argue about it, for she could see just the sort of book she wanted.

The book was almost as big as Emma, but she heaved it down from the shelf and looked inside. There were pictures of dogs of all shapes and sizes. There were pictures of feeding bowls and dog baskets and brushes and combs and collars and leads, and everything you needed to know about looking after a dog.

"What do you want that enormous thing for?" said Mum, as Emma carried the book to the counter to be stamped. "You can't even read."

"Yes I can," said Emma. "I can read my animal book at home."

Mum laughed. "Only because Dad has read it to you a hundred times," she said. "But you can look at the pictures, I suppose."

Emma was very busy for the next few weeks. Every day she looked at a new page in the big book, and every day she learned something new about dogs. She saved her pocket money until she had enough to buy a brush and a comb, and she brushed Muffin until he was almost bald.

She stopped having sweets and

crisps every time she went shopping with Mum, and Mum bought a tin of *Woofy Chunks* instead. Soon there was a big pile of tins in the larder, and Mum gave her an old soup plate to use as a feeding dish.

One Saturday, when Emma was out for a walk with Dad, she saw a notice on the door of the church hall.

"What does that say, Dad?" she asked.

"It says BOY SCOUTS' JUMBLE SALE," Dad told her.

"Can we go in?" said Emma.

"Why?" said Dad. "Do you want to buy a boy scout?"

"I want a second-hand basket for my dog," said Emma.

"You mean second-paw," said Dad, but he took Emma into the hall and helped her to find an almost-new basket for only fifty pence. Emma carried it home and put it on the floor in the kitchen.

"That's nice," said Mum. "All you need now is a blanket."

At school Emma was learning to knit. She asked her teacher to help her to knit a blanket for her dog's basket.

"What's that?" said Dad, when she brought it home.

"It's a blanket," said Emma. "I

knitted it all by myself. It's for my dog."

Dad laughed. "I thought it was a fishing net," he said. "It's got so many holes."

He gave Emma a packet of seeds. "Here, you can plant those for your dog," he said.

Emma looked at the packet. There was a picture of a cauliflower on the front.

"Dogs don't eat cauliflowers," she said.

"Collie dogs might," said Dad.

Emma sighed. Grown-ups could be silly sometimes.

One morning Emma put a bit of string round Muffin's neck and

9

took him for a walk down the path to the front gate.

"I don't think he wants to go for a walk," said the milkman.

"No," said Emma. "He keeps falling over. I expect it's because he hasn't got a proper collar and lead."

Next day when the milkman came he had a present for Emma. Emma opened it, and found a smart red lead and a brown leather collar.

"They're too small for my dog now," said the milkman. "Muffin can have them."

"Thank you," said Emma.

She put the collar and lead on Muffin. Muffin still fell over, but Emma didn't mind. Now she had everything she needed for her real dog, and there were only two more weeks to wait.

Emma's friend Katie was seven. She had a big black dog called Geordie, and every day after school she took him for a walk in the park. Every day Emma looked over the garden gate at Katie and Geordie going past.

"Can I come with you?" said Emma one afternoon. "I want to take my dog for a walk, too."

Katie looked at Muffin and laughed.

"You're not bringing that thing to the park," she said scornfully. "You can come with me when you've got a real dog." And she walked away.

Emma went to look at the calendar in the kitchen. Mum was there, making chips for tea.

"Only five more days," said Mum with a smile. "It's your birthday on Saturday." Emma danced round the kitchen. Five days wasn't very long at all.

Five days became four days, then three, then two, then one.

Then at last it was Saturday. Emma had lots of presents and cards. All of the cards had number six on them.

"NOW I am six!" said Emma.

Straight after breakfast Dad drove Emma to the Dogs' Home to choose her dog. There were big ones and little ones, fat ones and thin ones, smooth ones and furry ones. They were all so nice that

Emma didn't know which one to choose.

In the end it was a black and white spaniel which chose Emma. He jumped up at her and wagged his tail like mad.

"I'll have this one," said Emma. "I'm going to call him Fred."

"Why?" said Dad.

"Because that's his name," said Emma.

As soon as she got home, Emma gave Fred a bowl of *Woofy Chunks*. She brushed and combed him until his coat shone. Then she put his collar and lead on him and opened the back door.

"Where are you going, Emma?" said Mum.

"I'm taking Fred for a walk," said Emma.

Dad looked at Emma over the top of his newspaper.

"Oh no you're not," he said. "You're much too young to take a dog out all by yourself."

Emma sighed as she looked out of the window at Katie going by with Geordie.

"When will I be old enough?" she said in a small voice.

"When you are seven," said Mum and Dad together.

Mr and Mrs Pig's Evening Out

Mary Rayner

Once upon a time there lived a family of pigs. There was Father Pig and Mother Pig.

And then there were ten piglets. They were called Sorrel Pig, Bryony Pig, Hilary Pig, Sarah Pig, Cindy Pig, Toby Pig, Alun Pig, William Pig, Garth Pig and Benjamin Pig.

One evening Mother Pig called the children to her as they were playing all over the house. "Now piglets," she said, "your father and I are going out this evening."

There was a chorus of groans.

"Not far," said Mrs Pig, "and I've asked a very nice lady to come and look after you."

"What is her name?" asked William Pig.

"I don't like babysitters," said Benjamin.

"Oh," said Mrs Pig, looking vague, "well, she's coming from the agency so I'm not sure what her name is, but you're sure to like her."

"We didn't like the last one from the agency," grumbled Garth.

"I'm sure you'll find that this babysitter will be very nice. Now get along into your baths and I'll come and tuck you up before we go out."

The piglets took as long as they could having their baths and made a great many puddles and splashes in the bathroom, but at last Mother Pig got them upstairs.

Just as she was putting on her best dress, the front doorbell rang. Down ran Mrs Pig, grunting and puffing in her haste, to open the door.

A dark face peered at her,

heavily wrapped in a macintosh and hat.

"Are you Mrs Pig?" asked a gruff voice.

"Yes," said Mother Pig brightly. "Do come in. The children are just getting into their beds. They sleep in bunk beds," she explained, and so they did. Two to a bed, head to tail, stacked five beds high.

"Can you help me?" called Father Pig from the bedroom.

Mrs Pig hurried upstairs. He was just putting on his smart shirt which he always wore when they went out. It was dark blue, and Mrs Pig liked him to wear it because she thought it made him look thinner. Unfortunately the buttons *would* keep coming undone, so that everyone always noticed how very tight the shirt had become. Mrs Pig struggled to get it done up.

Suddenly she remembered that she had not asked the babysitter's name. She ran out of the bedroom again.

The babysitter was just settling herself comfortably on the sofa.

"Would you mind telling me what you are called?" said Mrs Pig. "The children do like to know."

"It's Mrs Wolf," said the babysitter, crossing a pair of dark

21

hairy legs and getting out her knitting.

"Oh thanks," said Mrs Pig, without thinking. "Now Mrs Wolf, I've left the kitchen light on and if you should feel like making yourself a hot drink or having something to eat later in the evening, do please help yourself."

"Thank you, I shall," said Mrs Wolf.

At that moment Mr Pig called through to say that he was quite ready, and with many farewell kisses and hugs for the children Mr and Mrs Pig went out for the evening with light hearts.

Mrs Wolf sat in the living room

and read magazines and knitted.
The piglets all seemed to have
gone off to sleep – she went
upstairs once to check. It seemed a
very long evening. There was
nothing to watch on television.

After a while Mrs Wolf began to
feel empty, so she went into the
kitchen. But she didn't turn on the
kettle. No. She turned on the *oven*.
Then she tiptoed up to the piglets'
bedroom.

In the lowest bunk bed were
Garth and Benjamin, snoring
faintly. Mrs Wolf looked longingly
at Garth, all rosy, plump and pink.

Then she snatched him up and
carried him off downstairs. He

made such a snorting and a
squealing that all his brothers and
sisters sat bolt upright in bed.
Whatever was going on?

Quick as a flash Sorrel cried,
"After him everyone, Mrs Wolf is
not to be trusted."

Seizing Garth's blanket off his
bed, the nine piglets galloped

downstairs as fast as their short legs would carry them.

They were in the nick of time. Mrs Wolf was bending over the oven with her back to them, holding Garth, about to put him in.

"Four of you take this side of the blanket, four that," hissed Sorrel outside the kitchen. The piglets did as they were told.

"Now!" ordered Sorrel. They ran in and threw the blanket over Mrs Wolf's head. She backed away from the oven still holding Garth. Muffled snarls came through the rug. The piglets held on tight. Mrs Wolf struggled and thrashed but

she could not get out. She dropped
Garth and went down on all fours.
Garth wriggled free. The piglets
hung on.

Mrs Wolf braced herself and
humped her back, her long hairy
tail lashing from side to side.
Terrible growls came from her.

"Hang on, everyone!" shouted
Sorrel. Mrs Wolf leaped into the
air. The piglets were tossed to and
fro but still they hung on bravely.

As soon as they were back on
their feet they circled round her so
that the rug was wrapped tighter
and tighter.

Then they tied the four corners
together so that she could not

possibly get out, and left her in the middle of the kitchen.

When their father and mother came home the ten piglets told them what a narrow escape they had had.

Father Pig went out into the night and carried the blanket bundle to the middle of the bridge. There he leaned over the parapet and shook Mrs Wolf into the swirling depths of the big river.

And she was not heard of again for a very long time.

One Very Small Foot

Dick King-Smith

"What animal has got only one foot?" said the children's father. "I bet you can't tell me."

"I can!" said Matthew and Mark with one voice. As well as looking exactly alike, the twins nearly always said exactly the same thing at exactly the same time. Matthew was ten minutes older than Mark, but after that there had never been the slightest difference between them.

"Go on then," said their father. "Tell me. What animal's got only one foot?"

"A chicken standing on one leg!" they said.

"That's silly," said Sophie seriously.

Sophie was four, a couple of years younger than her brothers.

"That's silly," she said. "It would still have a foot on the other leg. Anyway, Daddy, there isn't really an animal that's only got one foot, is there?"

"Yes, there is, Sophie."

"What?"

"A snail. Every snail has a big flat sticky muscle under it that it travels along on. That's called its foot. Next time you see a snail crawling along, pick it up carefully and turn it over, and you'll see. There are loads in the garden."

"Come on! Let's find one!" said Matthew to Mark and Mark to Matthew at the same time.

"Wait for me," said Sophie. But they didn't, so she plodded after them.

When she caught up with the twins, in a far corner of the garden, each was examining the underside of a large snail. Sophie was not surprised to see that the snails were also obviously twins, the same size, the same shape, the same striped greeny-browny colour.

"I know!" said Matthew.

"I know what you're going to say!" said Mark.

"Let's have a snail race!" they said.

"How are you going to tell them apart?" said Sophie.

"I know!" said Mark.

"I know what you're going to say!" said Matthew.

"Fetch us a felt pen, Sophie," they said.

"What are you going to do?" asked Sophie when she came back

with a red felt pen.

"Put my initial on my snail," said Mark and Matthew together.

"But you've got the same initial." The boys looked at each other.

"I know!" they said.

"I know what you're going to say," said Sophie, and she plodded off again. She came back with a blue felt pen.

After a moment, "Ready?" said Matthew, holding up his snail with a big red M on its shell, and at the same instant, "Ready?" said Mark, holding up his snail with a big blue M.

"Wait for me," said Sophie. "I haven't got a snail yet," but already the twins had set their twin snails side by side on the path that ran between the edge of the lawn and the flowerbed. The path was made of big oval flagstones, and they chose the largest one, perhaps a metre long. The far end of the flagstone was to be the winning-post.

"Ready, steady, go!" they shouted.

Sophie plodded off. "I'll beat them," she said. She was small but very determined.

Behind the first stone she moved, almost as though it had been waiting for her, was a snail. It was as different as possible from Red

M and Blue M. It was very little, no bigger than Sophie's middle fingernail, and it was a lovely buttercup yellow.

As she watched, it stretched out its head, poked out its two horns, and began to crawl, very slowly. It had a most intelligent face, Sophie thought. She picked it up carefully, and turned it over.

"What a very small-sized shoe you would take, my dear," she said. "I don't know whether you can win a race but you are very beautiful. You shall be my snail."

"Who won?" she said to Matthew and Mark when she returned.

"They didn't go the right way,"

they both said.

"But mine went furthest," they both said.

"No, it didn't," they both said.

They picked up their snails and put them side by side once more.

"Wait for me," Sophie said, and she put down the little yellow snail. It looked very small beside the others.

"Just look at Sophie's snail!" hooted the twins, but this time when they shouted, "Ready, steady, go!" neither Red M nor Blue M would move. They stayed stubbornly inside their shells and took not the slightest notice of their owners' cries of encouragement.

Sophie's snail plodded off.

It was small but very determined, and Sophie lay on the grass beside the path and watched it putting its best foot forward.

After half an hour, it reached the winning-post.

Sophie jumped up. "Mine's the winner!" she cried, but there was no one to hear.

The twins had become bored with snail-racing at exactly the same time and gone away. Red M and Blue M had gone away too, into the forest of the flowerbed. Only Sophie's snail kept stoutly on, while the straight silvery trail it had left glistened in the sunshine.

Sophie knelt down and carefully put her hand flat in front of the little yellow creature. It crawled solemnly on to it.

"What *have* you got in your hand, Sophie?" said her mother at tea time.

"It's Sophie's snail!" chorused Matthew and Mark.

"Put it straight out in the garden," said the children's mother.

"No," said Sophie in a small but determined voice.

Her mother looked at her, sighed, picked up a box of matches, emptied the matches out and gave Sophie the empty box.

"Put it in there till after tea," she said, "and go and wash your hands."

All that evening Sophie played with her snail. When it was bedtime, and she was ready to wash and do her teeth, she put the snail carefully on the flat rim of the washbasin.

Then (as she always did) she filled the basin with warm water right up to the overflow and washed her face and hands. The snail did not move, though it appeared to be watching.

Then (as she always did) she brushed her teeth very hard, making a lot of froth in her mouth and spitting the bubbly blobs of toothpaste out on top of the rather dirty water. She always liked doing this. The toothpaste blobs made strange shapes on the surface of the water, often like a map of the world. Tonight there was a big white Africa at one side of the basin.

Then (as she always did) she pulled the plug out, but as she turned to dry her hands the sleeve of her dressing gown scuffed the rim of the basin. Right into the middle of disappearing Africa fell a small yellow shape, and then the last of the whirlpooling frothing water disappeared down the plughole, leaving the basin quite empty.

Sophie plodded down the stairs.

"My snail's gone down the plughole," she said in a very quiet voice.

"You couldn't have kept it, you know," said her father gently. "It would have died anyway without its natural food."

"Next time you find one," said her mother, "just leave it in the garden. There are lots of other snails there, just as nice."

"Not as nice as my snail," said Sophie. She looked so unhappy that for once the twins said different things, in an effort to comfort her.

" 'Spect it died quickly," said Matthew.

"Sure to be drowned by now," said Mark.

*

Try as she would, Sophie could not stop herself thinking about what happened to you if you went down a plughole. She lay in bed and thought about the twins washing their hands in the basin and washing their teeth, and then later on Mum and Dad doing the same. All that water would be washing the body of her snail farther and farther away, down the drain into the sewer, down the sewer into the river, down the river into the sea.

When at last she slept, she dreamed that she was walking by the seaside, and there she saw, washed up on the beach, a familiar little yellow shape. But when she ran and picked it up, it had no head, no horns, no foot. It was just an empty snail shell.

Sophie woke early with the feeling that something awful had happened, and then she remembered what it was.

She plodded along to the bathroom and looked over the rim of the washbasin at the round plughole with its metal grating meant to stop things going down it.

"But you were too small," she said.

Leaning over as far as she could reach, she stared sadly into the black depths of the plughole. And as she stared, suddenly two little horns poked up through the grating, and then a head, and then a shell no bigger than her middle fingernail, a shell that was a lovely buttercup yellow.

Very carefully, Sophie reached out and picked up her small determined snail.

Very quietly she plodded down the stairs and opened the back door and went out into the garden and crossed the dewy lawn.

Very gently, at the exact spot she had found it, she put her snail down and watched it slowly move away on its very small foot.

"Goodbye, my dear," said Sophie.

"I hope we meet again," and then she sat happily on the wet grass watching, till at last there was nothing more to be seen of Sophie's snail.

Tracks

Ann Cameron

Julian had a book from the
library. By reading the book,
he was learning to be a tracker
and a guide and a scout. He had
shown it to Gloria. He wouldn't
show it to me.

"I could learn too," I said.

"You couldn't!" Julian said.

"I could too!" I said.

Julian shook his head. "A
tracker is strong and silent. You're

too little – and you talk all the time."

I hate it when Julian acts like that. It makes me want to fight him. But I didn't say one word. I just went away.

In the night I woke up and went downstairs. Julian's book was lying on the couch in the living room. I picked it up. I couldn't read it all, but I could see it was about tracks.

It had pictures of the hoof and paw prints of almost every kind of animal. It showed deer tracks and raccoon tracks, the tracks of zebras and giraffes and elephants.

I looked out of the living room

47

window. I could hear the wind. I could almost hear many animals outside. Very quietly I opened the front door and went out. I still had the book in my hand.

There was a full moon. I could see my own shadow on the grass, but I couldn't see any night animals. I looked for tracks, but there weren't any.

In real life I really had seen raccoon tracks once. I looked through Julian's book until I found some. I decided to copy them. I found a sharp stick and went to where our drive divides our lawn in two parts. The drive isn't paved. It's pebbly and sandy.

Raccoon tracks look almost like human hands, with narrow fingers and long sharp claws for fingernails. I stood on the grass and used my stick to copy them along the edge of the drive.

I walked on the grass to the street. Then I walked on the paved street to the other side of our drive. I copied more raccoon tracks on that side – so it looked like the raccoon had turned around and gone back to the street.

I hid my drawing stick in the hedge and went back in the house. I was careful not to leave any footprints. I put Julian's book back

on the couch, just the way he'd left it. I climbed the stairs, tiptoed past Mum and Dad's room, and went back to bed.

In the morning I went down to breakfast. Julian was running in the kitchen door with his book in his hand.

"Dad, Dad!" he shouted. "A raccoon was here last night!"

"Really?" my dad said. He went outside with Julian to study the tracks, and I went along.

Julian showed Dad his book. When Dad bent down to look at the tracks, I tried to look at Julian's book, too. But Julian wouldn't let me. Whenever I tried to, he covered it with his arm and poked me in the ribs with his elbow.

My dad stood up. "It sure does look like a raccoon was here!" he said. "Sometimes those little rascals come round to eat food out of rubbish bins. From now on, we'll need to keep the lids on tight."

The next night I woke up. I looked at the clock that sits on top of the brick on my night table. It was one a.m.

Julian was asleep with his pillow over his head. I went down to the living room.

I found his book on top of the TV

open to a page on African safaris. I went down to the basement and got my dad's hammer. I took it and the book outside. The moon was not quite as big as the night before, but there was plenty of light for working.

Every few feet I mashed up small spots of sandy ground with the hammer. Then I rounded them out just right.

I stood up and compared them to the picture in Julian's book. They looked the way they were supposed to – just like zebra tracks. Zebras leave hoof prints like horses. Their tracks are deeper in the ground than raccoon tracks. That's why I used the hammer.

In the morning, Julian was so excited he was yelling.

"Mum and Dad!! Huey! Come and look! There was a zebra here last night!"

We all ran outside. My dad studied Julian's book and the tracks.

"Hard to believe," my dad said, "but it sure does look that way!"

"Could it have been a horse?" my mum asked.

"All the horses around here have shoes," my dad said. "These tracks don't show shoe prints."

Gloria came over and saw the tracks. "Ama-a-a-zing!" she said.

She and Julian decided to make a zebra trap. They made the cage out of straight sticks tied together with rope. I brought them the rope from the cellar.

"We should put a carrot in the cage to attract the zebra," Gloria said. So Julian did.

He asked permission to sleep on the front porch, so he could watch for the zebra and catch it. Gloria got permission to stay the night and help.

Julian asked if I wanted to sleep downstairs with them to watch for the zebra. "We could take turns watching and sleeping," he said.

I said there wasn't room for three

of us on the porch. Besides, I was tired.

But in the night I woke up. I looked out of the bedroom window. The moon was not as big or as bright as the night before. I went to the cellar and got a hammer, a chisel and a flashlight. I crossed the living room on silent feet and peered out of the window to the porch.

Julian was on the floor in his sleeping bag with his pillow over his head. Gloria was sitting up with her back against the wall, facing the zebra cage. But her head was tipped over on her shoulder. She was asleep.

On tiptoe I went out on the porch. The porch has one board that squeaks. I didn't step on it. The tracking book just touched Julian's hand. I put the hammer, the chisel and the flashlight under my left arm. I was scared I would drop them. I bent down. Very carefully, I reached out with my right hand. Very gently, I took the book. Julian and Gloria did not wake up.

I walked to the zebra cage. I set my tools down on the grass.

Carrots are one of my favourite foods. I picked up the carrot in the cage. I bit off half and ate it. I used the flashlight to check the rest of the carrot for tooth marks I had made on the other half. I worked on them with my fingernail to make them look bigger. Then, I put the flashlight down and put the carrot back in the trap.

I used the hammer to make more zebra tracks – into the trap and back out again. I checked them with the light from the flashlight. They were OK. When I finished, I found a fallen pine bough. I used it to brush out all my own tracks.

I went to the edge of the street. At the edge of the street there is a narrow, sandy place. There was room for some very good tracks. Elephant tracks!

Elephants are really heavy. Their tracks sink in. I used the chisel to soften up the ground before I made the tracks with my hammer. I made fat, round tracks, with bumps for the toemarks – five each on the front feet and three on the back, just like the picture in Julian's book. Afterwards, I shone the flashlight on them. They looked good.

"The zebra was here!" Gloria said in the morning. "He was here – but I fell asleep. Huey! You should have helped us watch for him!"

"I'm too little," I said. "I'm afraid of zebras."

Julian and Gloria took my mum and dad and me outside and showed us the tracks – and the marks in the carrot.

My dad studied the carrot. "Those are tooth marks all right," he said.

My mum took the carrot and examined it. "Some kind of tooth marks . . ." she said, "But—" She never finished what she was going to say, because Julian was shouting and pointing at the street.

"There're more tracks out here! HUGE ones!"

We all went running to see.

"They look big enough to be

elephant tracks!" Gloria said.

My mum said, "What I don't understand is why all these animals are coming to our house. Do you have any ideas, Huey?"

Everybody looked at me. I had to say something.

"It's really strange!" I said.

I am a tracker and a scout. I am strong and I am silent. I know many things. But I keep them to myself.

Eddie and the Goat

Carolyn Haywood

Eddie was the youngest of the
four Wilson boys. There was
Rudy, aged twelve, the twins, Joe
and Frank, who were nine, and
Eddie. Eddie was seven.

Eddie was very fond of animals.
He often brought stray animals
home with him. Stray cats, stray
dogs, birds that had fallen out of
their nests, snails, snakes; anything
that was alive, Eddie loved.

For the past week the children in Eddie's class had been having the fun of owning a baby goat. A farmer who was a friend of Miss Weber, their teacher, had given the baby goat to her and she had brought it to school. The children had been reading the story of Heidi and they were all interested in Heidi's goat. Of course the children wanted the little goat to stay at school for ever, but Miss Weber said she would have to take it back to the farmer, because there really was no place to keep a goat.

"Couldn't we keep it where we have it now?" George asked. "At the back of the school on the grass?"

"Couldn't we build a house for it?" asked Eddie.

"No," said Miss Weber, "we can't keep the goat here. But the farmer said that if anyone would like to have the goat and would take proper care of it, he'd be glad to give it away."

Eddie could hardly believe his ears. "You mean for nothing?" he cried.

"That's what the farmer told me," said Miss Weber.

"Well, I could have it," said Eddie. "I could keep it at my house. I could take care of it."

"Are you sure, Eddie?" Miss Weber asked. "Are you sure your father and mother wouldn't object to your having a goat?"

"Oh, sure!" said Eddie. "My father and mother love goats. They'd be delighted to have a little goat."

"I think you had better ask them first," said Miss Weber.

"I don't have to ask them," said Eddie. "I can take the goat."

"Ask them first," said Miss Weber.

At dinner that night Eddie said, "Papa, you know the baby goat I told you about?"

65

Mr Wilson said, "What about the baby goat, Eddie?"

"Well, it's an awful nice little goat," said Eddie. "I could have a very enjoyable time with that little goat."

"A goat!" exclaimed Mr Wilson. "That's just what we need! A goat! Probably the only way we can ever get rid of the junk in the basement – get a goat to eat it!" And at this point Mr Wilson got up to go to a meeting. "Yes, indeed!" he said. "A goat is just what we need!"

The following day when Eddie went to school he said, "Miss Weber, I can have the goat. My father said it was just what we need."

"Very well, Eddie, the goat is yours," said Miss Weber. "Take it away this afternoon."

"I brought a dog collar and a lead," said Eddie. "Do you think she'll go with me?"

Miss Weber thought the goat would go with Eddie and it did. And a whole crowd of children went too. But Eddie had a hard time walking with the goat, because the goat was always walking sideways instead of forward. This made the going very slow and the children were always bumping into each other because the goat bumped into them. One by

one they left Eddie until he and
the goat were alone.

The closer Eddie got to his home
the more he thought of his father,
and the more he thought of his
father the more he felt that he was
not going to like the little goat.
There was something about the

way Father had said, "A goat is just what we need," that made Eddie feel perhaps he would not be pleased.

Eddie decided to sit down on the kerb and think the matter over. The goat lay down beside him. Here Mr Kilpatrick the policeman found them as he was driving home in his police car.

Mr Kilpatrick stopped and said, "What are you doing with that goat, Eddie?"

"I was taking her home but now I don't know. I am afraid perhaps my father won't like it." Then Eddie told Mr Kilpatrick how he had happened to get the goat.

"Did you ask your father whether you could bring the goat home?" Mr Kilpatrick asked.

"Well, not exactly," said Eddie. "I told him we had a goat at school and he said, 'That's just what we need, a goat!'"

"He did?" said Mr Kilpatrick, raising his eyebrows. "That doesn't sound too good to me."

"You don't think he'll like the goat, Mr Kilpatrick?" said Eddie, looking up at the big policeman.

Mr Kilpatrick shook his head. "I have me doubts," he said, "very grave doubts."

Eddie sat with his chin resting in the palm of his hand. The little goat nuzzled its nose under Eddie's arm. Eddie patted it on the head. "I think if my father knew this little goat, he would like her," he said.

"Maybe!" said Mr Kilpatrick. "But you made a big mistake in not talking to him about it first. You should have told him all the nice things about the goat and got him interested. You should have smoothed the way. That's what you call diplomacy. If you take this goat home now, your father will probably throw it out."

"Out where?" asked Eddie, with a startled face.

Mr Kilpatrick waved his arms

around. "Oh, he'll probably telephone for the RSPCA."

"What's that?" Eddie asked.

"The Royal Society for the Prevention of Cruelty to Animals," said Mr Kilpatrick.

"But I'm not going to be cruel to my goat," said Eddie.

"Nevertheless," said Mr Kilpatrick, "that's where it will go. You should have used diplomacy."

Eddie sat deep in thought. The goat was taking a nap. Mr Kilpatrick sat in his car, looking down at the two on the kerb.

In a few minutes Eddie looked up. His face was brighter. "Mr Kilpatrick," he said, "couldn't you keep my goat until I can use what you said on my father? I don't want my goat to go to the Cruelty to Animals."

"Oh, Mrs Kilpatrick wouldn't like it," said Mr Kilpatrick. "She wouldn't like it at all."

"But it would only be until tomorrow. I could talk to Papa tonight," said Eddie.

Mr Kilpatrick thought for a few minutes. Then he said, "Well, come on. We'll take it along. We'll see whether Mrs Kilpatrick will have it overnight."

Eddie got up and this woke the goat. He lifted it in his arms and put it on the front seat, between

Mr Kilpatrick and himself. In a moment they were off. They turned a few corners and the car stopped in front of Mr Kilpatrick's white fence.

Mrs Kilpatrick was cutting flowers in her garden. She looked up when the car stopped and waved her hand. She watched Mr Kilpatrick step out of the car and she watched Eddie step out. When she saw the goat, she said, "Now what in the name of peace are you bringing home?"

"It's just for the night, Katie," said Mr Kilpatrick. "I'm helping my friend Eddie here."

"It's my goat, Mrs Kilpatrick,"

said Eddie. "And Mr Kilpatrick says I have to talk to Papa, so he won't give it to the Cruelty to Animals. Mr Kilpatrick says I have to use – what kind of dip is it, Mr Kilpatrick?"

"Diplomacy," said Mr Kilpatrick.

"Well!" said Mrs Kilpatrick. "See that that goat is out of here tomorrow."

"It's all right, Katie," said Mr Kilpatrick. "It's just for tonight."

Mr Kilpatrick had a great big wooden box with a hinged lid. He turned it on its side and propped the lid open. "This will make a good house for a goat," he said. "I'll go over and get some straw from the stable and you won't have to worry about your goat. She'll be comfortable for the night."

"Thanks, Mr Kilpatrick," said Eddie. "Any time you want me to keep anything of yours I'll be glad to. Any turtles or anything."

"That's OK, Eddie," said Mr Kilpatrick. "Just talk to your father tonight. I'll bring the goat over tomorrow after school."

Eddie patted his goat on the head and ran off with a light heart.

When Eddie reached home, he told his brothers about the goat. They thought it would be wonderful to have a goat. "But I don't think Dad will let us have it," said Rudy.

"Well, just leave it to me," said Eddie. "I'm going to use dip . . . Well, anyway, I'm going to use it."

At dinner that evening Eddie said, "Papa, you know that goat we had in school?"

"Goat?" said his father. "Oh, yes! What about it?"

"Well, it's an awful nice goat," said Eddie.

"They smell terrible," said Mr Wilson.

"This one doesn't," said Eddie.

"Eddie," said his father, "if you are thinking of bringing that goat here, you can forget it right now."

"Oh, Papa!" Eddie groaned.

"I think it would be swell to have a goat," said Frank.

"We could harness it to the wagon and it could pull the groceries home for Mother," said Joe.

Eddie beamed on Joe. He began to think that Joe was smarter than Rudy.

"Goats give milk," said Rudy. "Good milk."

Mr Wilson looked at his four sons and said, "*No goat!*"

The next day when Mr Kilpatrick's car appeared in front of the Wilsons' house, Eddie ran out. "Here's your goat," said Mr

Kilpatrick. "Did you fix things up with your father?"

"Oh, Mr Kilpatrick!" cried Eddie. "I have to use some more dip . . . What kind of dip did you say it is?"

"Diplomacy!" Mr Kilpatrick shouted. "Diplomacy!"

"Well, I have to do it some more," said Eddie. "Will you keep the goat tonight?"

Mr Kilpatrick did not look as though he were going to keep the goat for five more minutes until Eddie said, "Please, Mr Kilpatrick, just tonight."

"OK!" said Mr Kilpatrick, "but you have to take her tomorrow.

Mrs Kilpatrick won't stand for it. That goat ate all the flowers in the front garden and Mrs Kilpatrick won't stand for it."

"Just tonight, Mr Kilpatrick," said Eddie. "Just tonight. Please."

Mr Kilpatrick drove off with the goat and that night at dinner Eddie said, "Papa, you know that goat we had at school?"

"Yes, Eddie," said his father. "What about the goat now?"

"Well, it's an awful nice goat," said Eddie.

"So you said before," said Mr Wilson.

"A goat would eat the grass and we wouldn't have to cut it so often," said Joe.

Mr Wilson looked round the table. "*No goat!*" he said. "Positively no goat!"

The following day was Saturday. After breakfast Eddie went over to Mr Kilpatrick's to see his goat. As he walked up the path from the front gate, Mrs Kilpatrick called out, "Eddie Wilson, you get that goat out of here! It ate up my flowers and this morning it ate up one of Mr Kilpatrick's woollen socks. You take that goat home with you."

"Oh, Mrs Kilpatrick!" said Eddie. "You'll have to keep it for me just one more night. I think my father likes the goat better every day and I think he will let me have it tomorrow."

"Well, if it eats up one more thing, out it goes," said Mrs Kilpatrick.

At lunch Eddie said, "Papa, you know that goat?"

"Yes, Eddie," said his father.

"Well, it's an awful nice goat," said Eddie.

Mr Wilson looked at Eddie's mother and they both laughed. "OK!" said Eddie's father. "But let me tell you this. If it smells, out it goes."

Eddie's face broke into a wide grin.

"Hurrah!" cried the twins.

"Swell!" shouted Rudy.

"Where is the goat?" Mr Wilson asked.

"It's over at Mr Kilpatrick's. He's keeping it for me."

When lunch was over, Eddie and his three brothers went over to Mr Kilpatrick's to get the goat. When they arrived, Eddie was carrying a package in his hand.

Mr Kilpatrick opened the door. "Papa says we can have the goat," said Eddie, "but only if it doesn't smell."

"Well, it doesn't smell much," said Mr Kilpatrick. "It's only billy-goats that smell real bad."

"I can fix that," said Eddie, opening his package. "I bought some scent at the store. It's gardenia."

When the little goat saw Eddie, she ran to meet him. "She knows me," Eddie cried, as he rubbed gardenia scent all over the goat.

There was a great deal of excitement over getting the goat to the Wilsons' because Mr Kilpatrick offered to give Eddie the big wooden box that had been the goat's house for the past two nights. It was too big to go into the boot of Mr Kilpatrick's car and for a while it looked as though the house could not be moved.

Then Eddie had an idea. "I know!" he said. "Let's see if Mr Ward will bring the fire engine over."

Mr Kilpatrick telephoned to Mr Ward, and about half an hour later Mr Wilson saw the fire engine stop in front of his house. On the front seat sat Mr Ward and Eddie with the goat between them and in the back were the other three boys with the big wooden box.

As Mr Wilson helped the boys to carry the box to the back of the garage, he said, "Phew!"

"What's the matter?" asked Eddie, looking frightened.

"I smell gardenia," said his father.

"Sure," said Eddie, "that's my goat. Nice, isn't it, Papa?"

And so they named Eddie's little goat Gardenia.

Elephant Big and Elephant Little

Anita Hewitt

Elephant Big was always boasting. "I'm bigger and better than you," he told Elephant Little. "I can run faster, and shoot water higher out of my trunk, and eat more, and—"

"No. You can't!" said Elephant Little.

Elephant Big was surprised.

Elephant Big was *always* right. Then he curled up his trunk and laughed and laughed.

"What's more, I'll show you," said Elephant Little. "Let's have a running race, and a shooting-water-out-of-our-trunks race, and an eating race. We'll soon see who wins."

"I shall, of course," boasted Elephant Big. "Lion shall be judge."

"The running race first!" Lion said. "Run two miles there and two miles back. One of you runs in the field, the other runs in the forest. Elephant Big shall choose."

Elephant Big thought and

thought, and Elephant Little pretended to talk to himself, "I hope he chooses to run in the field, because *I* want to run in the forest."

When Elephant Big heard this, he thought: "If Elephant Little wants very much to run in the forest, that means the forest is best." Aloud he said, "I choose the forest."

"Very well," said Lion. "One, two, three. Go!"

Elephant Little had short legs, but they ran very fast on the springy smooth grass of the field. Elephant Big had long, strong legs, but they could not carry him quickly along through the forest. Broken branches lay in his way; thorns tore at him; tangled grass caught at his feet. By the time he stumbled, tired and panting, back to the winning-post, Elephant Little had run his four miles, and was standing talking to Lion.

"What ages you've been!" said Elephant Little. "We thought you were lost."

"Elephant Little wins," said Lion.

Elephant Little smiled to himself.

"But I'll win the next race," said Elephant Big. "I can shoot water much higher than you can."

"All right!" said Lion. "One of you fills his trunk from the river, the other fills his trunk from the lake. Elephant Big shall choose."

Elephant Big thought and thought, and Elephant Little pretended to talk to himself, "I hope he chooses the river, because *I* want to fill my trunk from the lake."

When Elephant Big heard this, he thought: "If Elephant Little wants very much to fill his trunk from the lake, that means the lake is best." Aloud he said, "I choose the lake."

"Very well!" said Lion. "One, two, three. Go!"

Elephant Little ran to the river and filled his trunk with clear, sparkling water. His trunk was small, but he spouted the water as high as a tree.

Elephant Big ran to the lake, and filled his long, strong trunk with water. But the lake water was

heavy with mud, and full of slippery, tickly fishes. When Elephant Big spouted it out, it rose only as high as a middle-sized thorn bush. He lifted his trunk and tried harder than ever. A cold little fish slipped down his throat, and Elephant Big spluttered and choked.

"Elephant Little wins," said Lion.

Elephant Little smiled to himself.

When Elephant Big stopped coughing, he said, "But I'll win the next race, see if I don't. I can eat much more than you can."

"Very well!" said Lion. "Eat where you like and how you like."

Elephant Big thought and thought, and Elephant Little pretended to talk to himself, "I must eat and eat as fast as I can, and I mustn't stop; not for a minute."

Elephant Big thought to himself: "Then I must do exactly the same. I must eat and eat as fast as I can, and I mustn't stop; not for a minute."

"Are you ready?" asked Lion. "One, two, three. Go!"

Elephant Big bit and swallowed, and bit and swallowed, as fast as he could, without stopping. Before very long, he began to feel full up inside.

Elephant Little bit and swallowed, and bit and swallowed. Then he stopped eating and ran round a thorn bush three times. He felt perfectly well inside.

Elephant Big went on biting and swallowing, biting and swallowing, without stopping. He began to feel very, very funny inside.

Elephant Little bit and swallowed, and bit and swallowed. Then again he stopped eating, and ran round a thorn bush six times. He felt perfectly well inside.

Elephant Big bit and swallowed, and bit and swallowed, as fast as he could, without stopping once,

until he felt so dreadfully ill inside
that he had to sit down.

Elephant Little had just finished
running around a thorn bush nine
times, and he still felt perfectly
well inside. When he saw Elephant
Big on the ground, holding his
tummy and groaning horribly,

Elephant Little smiled to himself.

"Oh, I do like eating, don't you?" he said. "I've only just started. I could eat and eat and eat and eat."

"Oh, oh, oh!" groaned Elephant Big.

"Why, what's the matter?" asked Elephant Little. "You look queer. Sort of green! When are you going to start eating again?"

"Not a single leaf more!" groaned Elephant Big. "Not a blade of grass, not a twig can I eat!"

"Elephant Little wins," said Lion.

Elephant Big felt too ill to speak.

After that day, if Elephant Big began to boast, Elephant Little smiled, and said, "Shall we have a running race? Shall we spout water? Or shall we just eat and eat and eat?"

Then Elephant Big would remember. Before very long, he was one of the nicest, most friendly elephants ever to take a mud bath.

Milly-Molly-Mandy Minds a Baby

Joyce Lankester Brisley

*Milly-Molly-Mandy is a little girl
who lives in a cottage in the country
with her Mother, Father, Grandma,
Grandpa, Aunty and Uncle. She has
a friend called Susan who lives
close by. This story is about what
happened when Milly-Molly-Mandy
found a tiny baby one day.*

*

Once upon a time Milly-Molly-Mandy had to mind a tiny little baby.

It was the funniest, tiny little baby you could possibly imagine, and Milly-Molly-Mandy had to mind it because there didn't seem to be anybody else to do so. She couldn't find its mother or its father or any of its relations, so she had to take it home and look after it herself (because, of course, you can't leave a tiny little baby alone in a wood, with no one anywhere about to look after it).

And this is how it happened.

Milly-Molly-Mandy wanted some

acorn-cups (which are useful for making dolls' bowls, and wheels for matchbox carts, and all that sort of thing, you know). So, as little-friend-Susan was busy looking after her baby sister, Milly-Molly-Mandy went off to the woods with just Toby the dog to look for some.

While she was busy looking she heard a loud chirping noise. And Milly-Molly-Mandy said to herself, "I wonder what sort of bird that is?" And then she found a ripe blackberry, and forgot about the chirping noise.

After a time Milly-Molly-Mandy said to herself, "How that bird does keep on chirping?" And then Toby the dog found a rabbit-hole, and Milly-Molly-Mandy forgot again about the chirping noise.

After some more time Milly-Molly-Mandy said to herself, "That bird sounds as if it wants something." And then Milly-Molly-Mandy went towards a brambly clearing in the wood from which the chirping noise seemed to come.

But when she got there the chirping noise didn't seem to come from a tree, but from a low bramble-bush. And when she got to the low bramble-bush the chirping noise stopped.

Milly-Molly-Mandy thought that

was because it was frightened of her. So she said out loud, "It's all right – don't be frightened. It's only me!" just as kindly as she could, and then she poked about in among the bramble-bush. But she couldn't find anything, except thorns.

And then, quite suddenly, lying in the grass on the other side of the bramble-bush, Milly-Molly-Mandy and Toby the dog together found what had been making all the chirping noise. It was so frightened that it had rolled itself into a tight little prickly ball, no bigger than the penny indiarubber ball which Milly-Molly-Mandy

had bought at Miss Muggins's
shop the day before.

For what *do* you think it was? A
little tiny weeny baby hedgehog!

Milly-Molly-Mandy *was* excited.
And so was Toby the dog! Milly-
Molly-Mandy had to say, "No,
Toby! Be quiet, Toby!" very firmly
indeed. And then she picked up
the baby hedgehog in a bracken
leaf (because it was a very prickly
baby, though it was so small), and
she could just see its little soft
nose quivering among its prickles.

Then Milly-Molly-Mandy looked
about to find its nest (for, of
course, she didn't want to take it
away from its family), but she

couldn't find it. And then the baby began squeaking again for its mother, but its mother didn't come.

So at last Milly-Molly-Mandy said comfortingly, "Never mind, darling – I'll take you home and look after you!"

So Milly-Molly-Mandy carried the baby hedgehog between her two hands very carefully; and it unrolled itself a bit and quivered its little soft nose over her fingers as if it hoped they might be good to eat, and it squeaked and squeaked, because it was very hungry. So Milly-Molly-Mandy hurried all she could, and Toby the dog capered along at her side and at last they got home to the nice white cottage with the thatched roof.

Father and Mother and Grandpa and Grandma and Uncle and Aunty were all very interested indeed.

Mother put a saucer of milk on the stove to warm, and then they tried to feed the baby. But it was too little to lap from a saucer, and it was too little even to lick from Milly-Molly-Mandy's finger. So at last they had to wait until it opened its mouth to squeak and then squirt drops of warm milk into it with Father's fountain-pen filler!

After that the baby felt a bit
happier, and Milly-Molly-Mandy
made it a nest in a little box of
hay. But when she put it in it
squeaked and squeaked again for
its nice warm mother till Milly-
Molly-Mandy put her hand in the
box; and then it snuggled up
against it and went to sleep. And

Milly-Molly-Mandy stood there and chuckled softly to herself, because it felt so funny being mistaken for Mrs Hedgehog! (She quite liked it!)

When Father and Grandpa and Uncle came in to dinner the baby woke and began squeaking again. So Uncle picked it up in his big hand to have a look at it, while Milly-Molly-Mandy ran for more milk and the fountain-pen filler.

And the baby squeaked so loudly that Uncle said, "Hul-lo, Horace! What's all this noise about?" And Milly-Molly-Mandy was pleased, because "Horace" just seemed to suit the baby hedgehog, and no one knew what its mother had named it (but I don't suppose it was Horace!).

Milly-Molly-Mandy was kept very busy all that day feeding Horace every hour or two. He was so prickly that she had to wrap him round in an old handkerchief first – and he looked the funniest little baby in a white shawl you ever did see!

When bedtime came Milly-Molly-Mandy wanted to take the hedgehog's box up to her little room with her. But Mother said no, he would be all right in the kitchen till morning. So they gave him a hot water bottle to snuggle against (it was an ink-bottle wrapped in flannel), and then Milly-Molly-Mandy went off to bed.

But being "mother" even to a hedgehog is a very important sort of job, and in the night Milly-Molly-Mandy woke up and thought of Horace, and wondered if he felt lonely in his new home.

And she creepy-crept in the dark to the top of the stairs and listened.

And after a time she heard a tiny little "Squeak! squeak!" coming from the kitchen. So she hurried and pulled on her dressing-gown and her bedroom slippers, and then she hurried and creepy-crept in the dark downstairs into the kitchen, and carefully lit the candle on the dresser.

And then she fed Horace and talked to him in a comfortable whisper, so that he didn't feel lonely any more. And then she put him back to bed and blew out the candle, and creepy-crept in the dark upstairs to her own little bed. (And it did feel so nice and warm to get into again!)

Next day Horace learned to open his mouth when he felt the fountain-pen filler touch it (he couldn't see, because his eyes weren't open yet – just like a baby

puppy or kitten). And quite soon
he learned to suck away at the
filler just as if it were a proper
baby's bottle! And he grew and
grew, and in a week's time his eyes
were open. And soon he grew little
teeth, and could gobble bread and
milk out of an egg-cup, and
sometimes a little bit of meat or
banana.

He was quite a little-boy
hedgehog now, instead of a little
baby one, and Milly-Molly-Mandy
didn't need to get up in the night
any more to feed him.

Milly-Molly-Mandy was very
proud of him, and when little-
friend-Susan used to say she had

to hurry home after school to look after her baby sister, Milly-Molly-Mandy used to say she had to hurry too to look after the baby Horace. She used to give him walks in the garden, and laugh at his funny little back legs and tiny tail as he waddled about, nosing the ground. When Toby the dog barked he would roll himself up into a prickly ball in a second; but he soon came out again, and would run to Milly-Molly-Mandy's hand when she called "Horace!" (He was quite happy with her for a mother.)

One day Horace got out of his hay-box in the kitchen, and they

couldn't find him for a long time,
though they all looked – Father
and Mother and Grandpa and
Grandma and Uncle and Aunty
and Milly-Molly-Mandy. But at
last where do you think they found
him? – in the larder!

"Well!" said Uncle, "Horace
knows how to look after himself
all right now!"

After that Horace's bed was put
out in the barn, and Milly-Molly-
Mandy would take his little basin
of bread and milk out to him, and
stay and play till it got too chilly.

And then, one frosty morning,
they couldn't find Horace
anywhere, though they all looked

– Father and Mother and Grandpa and Grandma and Uncle and Aunty and Milly-Molly-Mandy. But at last, a day or two after, Grandpa was pulling out some hay for the pony Twinkletoes, when what do you think he found! A little ball of prickles cuddled up deep in the hay!

Horace had gone to sleep for the winter, like the proper little hedgehog he was! (Grandpa said that sort of going to sleep was called "hibernating".)

So Milly-Molly-Mandy put the hay with the prickly ball inside it into a large box in the barn, with a little bowl of water nearby (in case

Horace should wake up and want a drink).

And there she left him (sleeping soundly while the cold winds blew and the snows fell) until he should wake up in the spring and come out to play with her again!

(And that's a true story!)

The Dog Who Frightened the Sea

Dorothy Edwards

There was once a corgi-dog called Peter who lived with a boy and girl called Jane and Frank.

One day they all went to the seaside for a holiday. They stayed in a white house that was very near the sea. There were three white steps going up to the front door, and inside the front door was a slippery hall with rugs on it. When they arrived, Peter ran straight up those steps and through that door, sent the rugs flying, and slipped and slithered right to the foot of the stairs.

"What do they want to come to a slidy place like this for?" he grumbled.

He grumbled when they went down on to the beach. He could see that Jane and Frank thought it was a lovely place, but he couldn't understand why. It was sandy and stony and there was all that nasty salty moving water!

"I wish we had stayed in our own

home," he said to himself. "I like our house where the floors aren't slidy, and the garden where there is nice brown earth and green grass and where the water lives in taps."

But Jane and Frank only laughed at him.

"This sand-stuff won't even make me properly dirty," he grumbled, and he rolled about in it to try, and Jane and Frank laughed more than ever.

So he settled himself down with his nose on his front paws and looked hard at the sea.

Soon the children were running along the water's edge, jumping when the little waves rushed at their feet. They watched the coloured seaweed riding in on top of the big waves, and when the sea went back a little they ran in, snatched up the seaweed and ran along the beach with it.

"Come on, Peter Corgi," they said, "come and play!"

"Ah now, that looks like fun," said Peter, and he jumped up and rushed down the beach towards them, and tried to catch the seaweed in their hands. As they ran he bounced along beside them. Now he was happy!

But oh dear! Jane and Frank ran on and on, straight into that

dreadful sea! Peter only just
stopped himself in time, right on
the edge of the water! He stood
there and stared at the rushing
tumbling waves. He saw those big
waves coming in over and over
each other and he didn't like them.

"O-O-O-O—" he said out loud.

"Come on, Corgi," said Jane, "it's lovely!"

But Peter didn't move. He stared and stared at that water that wouldn't stay still. He put back his ears and stuck his feet into the wet sand, and made a whiny-piny noise that meant: "Come out! Come out!" But Jane and Frank only laughed and splashed at him, so he turned and ran back to the house. Up the steps he went, skitter-scatter among the rugs, then up the stairs where he hid himself under Frank's bed.

After that the children tried very hard to make Peter like the sea. Sometimes Frank threw a ball for

Peter to bring back to him. Peter would dash across the sand and fetch the ball and bring it back wagging his stumpy tail with the greatest pleasure. But when Frank threw it into the sea and said, "Get it! Good dog!" he pretended that he didn't know where it had gone, and ran up and down the beach as if he were looking for it among the stones.

When the children went into the sea to bathe he tried to make them come out. He ran along the edge of the sea with the ball in his mouth, and now and again he dropped it, and sat beside it, and looked to see if Jane and Frank were coming out to play with him. When they took no notice he ran along the beach barking at the waves and showing his teeth at them.

"I wish he would come in the water and play with us," the children said.

But their mother said, "Don't worry him, he'll come when he wants to."

So Peter went on not liking the sea. He was very jealous of those big waves that Jane and Frank seemed to like so much. "Great big fidgety things," he growled.

Then one afternoon a strange thing happened. The children were playing with a little boat and jumping and splashing in the water. It was a nice little boat with white sails and they were so pleased with it they didn't notice an extra big wave come curling over the sea. Peter did though!

He sat up and watched it as it came rolling in, and, as it came "whoosh" it picked up the little boat and flung it on to the sand, and at the same time – "whoosh" – it tumbled Jane and Frank over. How they laughed!

But Peter was very cross! That bad old sea had tumbled his children over! He jumped up barking and barking. He tore straight down the beach, straight into the waves and BIT THE SEA.

Oh, it did taste nasty! And a piece of slippery seaweed got tangled in his teeth. But he was so cross, he bit and barked and growled and grumbled until another wave came along and tumbled *him* over too.

The children came out of the water and stared at him as he came out and shook himself. He began to make growly noises.

"Why," said Jane, "he's growling at the sea!" And she put her arm round his wet furry neck. "Silly dog!" she said.

"Grrh-rh-rh," said Peter to the

sea, and that meant, "I'll bite you again if you don't behave yourself!"

And would you believe it – slowly, slowly the sea began to go away as the little dog ran up and down the beach in front of it! "Woof-woof! Be off," he barked.

The waves still crept in but each wave was a little smaller than the one before. The big waves had gone already. Soon Peter saw the wet sand and the seaweed drying in the sunshine and the new pink shells laid bare on the shore.

"Ah-ha," barked the corgi-dog, wagging his tiny stumpy tail, "it's going because it's frightened of ME."

He was so proud, he stopped being cross. "Woof, woof," he barked, "I'm not afraid of you," and into the sea he ran. He began to swim to and fro, barking and barking.

"It's going away because I told it

to. Look, Jane and Frank, the sea's afraid of ME!"

The children ran to where their mother was sitting.

"Look, look," they said. "Look at Peter! He doesn't mind the sea now."

"Indeed he doesn't," their mother told them. "I suppose that's because the tide is turning."

But Peter didn't know that. He thought the sea was going because it was afraid of him.

Fox's Revenge

Andrew Matthews

Wolf lived alone in a house on
Shady Lane. He was long
and lean, and his fur was as grey
as smoke. His green eyes seemed to
burn, and he had a wide, hungry
smile. On nights when the moon
was full, Wolf went out into his
garden to howl, and the sound
made the whole of Boggart Hollow
shiver. Wolf would have been a
fearsome beast indeed, if it hadn't

been for his tail. It was as bald as a pebble.

When Wolf walked down the street, the other animals nodded to him respectfully, but after he passed by, they turned to look at his bald pink tail and they giggled. "I wonder where his fur went?" they asked each other, but no one seemed to know.

This is how it happened.

One fine, frosty winter's morning, Wolf went out for a slink down Shady Lane. He hadn't gone far when he met Fox coming the other way. Fox was carrying a pie that he'd filched from a kitchen windowsill. The pie was still

warm, and it steamed in the cold
air. It smelled so delicious that
Wolf's stomach began to gurgle.

"Good morning, Fox!" said Wolf,
gazing at the pie with his great
green eyes.

"G-good morning," Fox said
nervously, staring at Wolf's

long fangs.

"That's a fine-looking pie," said Wolf. "I wonder if it tastes as good as it looks?"

"Why not try some and find out?" said Fox. He broke off a small piece of the pie and gave it to Wolf.

Wolf chewed and swallowed, and licked his whiskers.

"How does it taste?" asked Fox.

"Hard to tell from such a little piece," Wolf said slyly.

Fox was quick to take the hint. He broke the pie in two and gave half of it to Wolf.

"Hmm!" said Wolf, talking with his mouth full. "I still can't seem to make up my mind. Perhaps I should have another taste, just to make sure."

With a heavy sigh, Fox handed over the rest of the pie and watched sulkily as it disappeared down Wolf's greedy throat.

"It was as good as it looked after all," said Wolf, as he licked the last few crumbs from the tip of his nose. "A very fine pie indeed!" He walked off, laughing to himself at the way he had got the better of Fox.

Fox was furious. "No one tricks me and gets away with it!" he growled quietly. "I'll show you a thing or two about cunning, you big bully!"

A few nights later, Wolf was dozing in an armchair by the fire when a knock came at his door. It was Fox, wearing a smile that was as slippery as satin. "My dear fellow!" Fox exclaimed. "I was just passing, and I wondered if you would care to join me. The duck pond has frozen over, and there's a splendid view of the full moon from the middle of it. We can look at the moon together and you can howl while I yap."

"What a kind thought!" said Wolf. "I haven't had a good howl in ages."

Fox and Wolf strolled to the

duck pond, and when he reached the edge, Fox sniffed. "I smell cheese!" he said.

"I can't," said Wolf.

"I know cheese when I smell it, and I smell it now," Fox insisted. He took two steps on to the frozen pond and barked, "Look!"

There, in the middle of the pond, was the moon's reflection, as round and yellow as a Cheddar cheese. Wolf ran over and tried to take a bite, but he bumped his nose against the cold, hard ice. "Ow!" he yelped. "It's frozen into the ice. How can we get at it?"

Fox walked round the reflection, pretending to think hard. "I'll run back to my cottage for an axe," he said at last. "We'll chop out that cheese in no time. You stay here, and cover the cheese with your tail so that no one else finds it."

"Good thinking!" said Wolf. He sat on the ice and spread out his tail.

Fox hurried off towards his cottage, but as soon as he was out of sight round a corner, he sneaked back and hid behind a tree so that he could watch Wolf.

It grew colder and colder. Wolf's bottom got number and number, until he couldn't feel it at all. "Where has Fox got to?" he grumbled. "It feels as if I've been waiting here for hours!"

Just then, Fox called out, "Hunters are coming! Hunters are coming!"

Wolf panicked. He tried to run away, but something held him back, and his claws screeched on

the ice. He turned his head and saw that his tail had stuck to the surface of the pond.

"Hunters are coming!" Fox shouted again.

Wolf heaved with all his strength. There was a ripping sound, and suddenly he was free. He ran straight home and shut all his doors and windows. Only when he turned the last lock did he notice how peculiar his tail felt. He tried to swish it, but it only wiggled. Wolf glanced over his shoulder and saw that he had left all the fur from his tail stuck to the ice on the pond.

Wolf never found out that Fox

had tricked him. Indeed, he was terribly grateful to Fox, and when they next met, Wolf shook Fox by the paw. "If it hadn't been for you, Fox, those hunters might have caught me!" Wolf said.

"Yes, but it's a shame about your tail," said Fox.

"I know," Wolf agreed sadly. "But it's better to lose the hair from your tail than lose your life."

"Fur better!" said Fox, and his eyes twinkled like frosty stars.

The Runaway Reptiles

Margaret Mahy

Sir Hamish Hawthorn, the famous old explorer, was not happy.

"Oh, Marilyn," he cried to his favourite niece. "I long to go exploring up the Orinoco river once more, but who will look after my pets?"

"The Reverend Crabtree next door will feed the cats, I'm sure," said Marilyn. "He is a very kind-hearted man. And I will take care of the alligator for you."

"But Marilyn," Sir Hamish said, "what about your neighbour? He might object to alligators."

Marilyn lived in Marigold Avenue – a most respectable street. The house next door was exactly the same as hers. It had the same green front door, the same garden and the same marigolds. A man called Archie Lightfoot lived there. He was rather handsome, but being handsome was not everything. Would he enjoy having a twenty-foot Orinoco alligator next door?

"Don't worry, Uncle dear," said

Marilyn. "I shall work something out."

At that exact moment, by a curious coincidence, Archie Lightfoot was opening an important-looking letter.

Dear Mr Lightfoot, he read. *Your great-aunt – who died last week – has left you her stamp album, full of rare and valuable stamps.*

"Terrific!" shouted Archie. Though he had never met his great-aunt, he had inherited her great love of stamps. Now, it seemed, he had inherited her stamp album as well. He read on eagerly.

There is one condition. You must give a good home to your aunt's twenty-foot Nile crocodile. If you refuse, you don't get the stamp collection. Those are the terms of the will.

"What will Marilyn Hawthorn say?" muttered Archie Lightfoot. "A beautiful girl like that will not want a twenty-foot Nile crocodile on the lawn next door. I will have to work something out."

That night, Marilyn Hawthorn tossed and turned. She could not sleep. In the end she decided to get up and make herself some toast. She could see the light next door shining on the marigolds. Archie Lightfoot was evidently having something to eat as well.

There is something about midnight meals that makes people have clever ideas. Sure enough, on the stroke of twelve, Marilyn Hawthorn suddenly thought of the answer to her problem.

The next day she ran up a large blue sun bonnet and a pretty shawl on her sewing machine, and borrowed the biggest motorised wheelchair she could find. Then she went round to her uncle's house.

Before leaving for the Orinoco, Uncle Hamish helped his niece settle the alligator comfortably in the wheelchair, packing it in with lots of wet cushions. The big sun bonnet nearly hid its snout, but Marilyn made it wear sunglasses to help the disguise.

"I shan't forget this," Sir Hamish said in a deeply grateful voice.

"Neither shall I," murmured Marilyn, wheeling the alligator out into the street.

As Marilyn pushed the disguised alligator through her front gate she noticed Archie Lightfoot pushing a large motorised wheelchair through his front gate, too. Sitting in it was someone muffled in a scarf, a floppy hat and sunglasses.

"My old grandfather is coming to live with me for a while," Archie said with a nervous laugh.

"How funny!" said Marilyn. "My old granny is coming to stay with *me*."

The two old grandparents looked at each other through their sunglasses and grinned toothily.

"Unfortunately," Archie added quickly, "my old grandfather can sometimes be very crabby. He has a big heart, but occasionally he

works himself up into a bad temper. Do warn your grandmother not to talk to him."

"I have the same problem with Granny," Marilyn replied. "She is basically big-hearted, but at times she can be bad-tempered. If you try to talk to her when she's hungry, she just snaps your head off!"

At first, things went smoothly. Every day Marilyn gave the alligator a large breakfast of fish and tomato sauce. Then she tucked the huge reptile into the wheelchair with blankets soaked in homemade mud. Next, she wheeled it into the garden and settled it down with a bottle of cordial, an open tin of sardines and the newspaper. The alligator always looked eagerly over the fence to see what was going on next door.

In his garden, Archie Lightfoot was settling his old grandfather down with tuna fish sandwiches and a motoring magazine. His grandfather blew a daring kiss to Marilyn Hawthorn's grandmother. Marilyn saw her alligator blow one back.

"You are not to blow kisses to a respectable old gentleman," she said sternly. The grandfather blew another kiss and the alligator did the same. Marilyn smacked its paw. It tried to bite her, but she was much too quick for it.

While Marilyn Hawthorn and Archie Lightfoot were at work, the two old grandparents blew kisses to one another and tossed fishy snacks across the fence.

That evening, when Marilyn Hawthorn got home, she noticed that her alligator seemed rather ill. It sighed a great deal, and merely toyed with its sardines at supper. Marilyn felt its forehead. It was warm and feverish, a bad thing in alligators, which are, of course, cold-blooded. She took it to the vet at once.

"What on earth is this?" cried the vet, listening to the alligator's heart. "This alligator is in love!"

The alligator sighed so deeply it accidentally swallowed the vet's thermometer.

"It must be homesick for the Orinoco," Marilyn thought to herself. So she took a day off work, wrapped cool mudpacks around the alligator, and put it in the marigold garden – with a large photograph of the Orinoco river to look at.

As she was doing this, Archie Lightfoot's face appeared over the garden fence.

"Oh, I'm so worried about my

grandfather," he cried. "I have had to take him to the vet – I mean, the doctor – and he sighed so deeply that he swallowed a stethoscope."

"And I've had to take the day off work to look after my old granny," said Marilyn. "*She* has swallowed a thermometer."

"Ahem!" coughed Archie Lightfoot, clearing his throat nervously. "Perhaps, since you are taking the day off work, you might like to slip over and see my stamp collection."

"I'd love to," replied Marilyn.

Marilyn Hawthorn and Archie Lightfoot spent rather a long time looking at the stamp collection.

They forgot their responsibilities. But when they switched on the radio, they were alarmed to hear the following announcement:

"We interrupt this programme to bring you horrifying news. Two twenty-foot saurians – crocodiles, or perhaps they are alligators – both wearing sunglasses, are driving down the main road in motorised wheelchairs."

"Oh, no!" cried Archie Lightfoot. "Oh, no!" cried Marilyn Hawthorn. Together, they ran outside. Their two lawns were quite empty.

"This is serious," gasped Marilyn. "Oh, Mr Lightfoot, I must confess that my grandmother is really an alligator!"

"And my old grandfather's a crocodile," cried Archie Lightfoot. "I didn't dream that a lovely woman like you could be fond of reptiles."

"We can discuss that later," said Marilyn briskly. "First, we must get our dear pets back."

Quickly, they climbed into Marilyn's sports car and took off after the runaway reptiles. They soon saw them whizzing along in their wheelchairs. Overhead, a police helicopter hovered, with several policemen and the vet inside it.

"It's very strange," said Marilyn, "but they seem to be heading for my uncle's house. I do wish Uncle Hamish were at home. He would know what to do in a case like this."

The runaways turned into the street where Marilyn's uncle lived, but they did not turn in at his gate. Instead, they went through the next-door gateway, straight to the home of the Reverend Crabtree.

Imagine Marilyn's surprise when she saw her Uncle Hamish sitting on the verandah, showing the Reverend Crabtree his souvenirs of the Orinoco.

"Uncle, I didn't know you were back!" she exclaimed.

"Well, I have only just returned," he said, looking in amazement at the two reptiles. "The Orinoco wasn't as good as I remembered it, so I came home early. But Marilyn, why has my alligator split itself in two?"

"Oh, Uncle, this is not another alligator – it's a crocodile. And it belongs to Archie Lightfoot," Marilyn explained. "These two bad reptiles ran away together in their wheelchairs and came here."

By now the police helicopter had landed on the lawn, and the policemen, followed by the vet, came running over.

"Don't hurt those saurians," the vet was shouting. "They are not very well. They are in love!"

"Ah," said the Reverend Crabtree. "I understand! They have eloped and wish to get married."

The crocodile and the alligator swished their tails and snapped their jaws as one reptile, to show he was right.

"I'm not sure if I, a minister of the church, should marry an alligator and a crocodile," said the Reverend Crabtree doubtfully. "It doesn't seem very respectable."

"But it seems a pity to miss out on the chance of marrying two creatures so clearly in love," said Archie. Then, turning to Marilyn he added, "Suppose we get married, too. Will that make it more respectable? After all, we did bring these two reptiles together. It's only fair that they should do the same for us!"

So Marilyn Hawthorn married Archie Lightfoot, and the crocodile and the alligator were married too. Sir Hamish gave both brides away. Then he swapped over and became best man to the two bridegrooms.

Marilyn and Archie turned their

two little houses into one large house, and their lawns into a swimming pool for the two saurians. And they lived happily ever after, even though they had to begin every morning of their lives together feeding sardines to a handsome Nile crocodile and an Orinoco alligator – both with big hearts and even bigger appetites.

Sarah Squirrel's Triumph

John Cotton

Sarah Squirrel was cross. Her bushy tail shook with annoyance. That "Mum" had done it again!

Sarah knew the lady was called Mum because she had heard the children in the garden call out, "Mum, Mum! Look at this." Mum would come out to look at a blue tit showing off by hanging upside down to eat some nuts. It was those very nuts that were the cause of Sarah Squirrel's annoyance.

At first Mum had put out some nuts for the birds on the bird table in the front garden. It only seemed fair to Sarah that she should have some too. So Sarah made a quick climb up the pole that held up the table, then scampered on to the table itself for a tasty meal.

"Oh dear!" Mum had said. "Those nuts were meant for the birds, not the squirrels. I will have to do something about it."

What Mum did was to hang the nuts in a little box from a branch of a tree in the garden. The box was made of wire mesh; the holes were just big enough for the birds' little beaks to peck at the nuts inside.

Sarah Squirrel had no difficulty in climbing the tree and down the string to reach the box. The wire mesh was a bit of a nuisance because it made eating the nuts a rather slow business. So Sarah bit through the string so that the box fell to the ground where the lid burst open. Sarah could then easily eat the nuts that had spilled out.

"Drat that squirrel!" Mum had said. "I will have to find another way to stop her eating the birds' nuts."

163

Sarah thought this was most
unfair. It was all right for the
birds, most of them flew south for
the winter. Some even flew as far
as Africa where it was even
warmer. But she had to stay in the
garden all through the winter. She
spent most of it sleeping, it was
true. But if there was a warm day

she could wake up. Then she would feel like a snack.

So she had to build up a little store of food during the summer in readiness for that. So Sarah thought she deserved a share of the nuts because she had to think of winter as well. Just because the birds were pretty and showed off a lot was no excuse. Didn't she have a pretty brown face and a lovely bushy tail?

What Mum did next was to hang a little box of nuts from a string in the middle of the washing line. Sarah smiled at this. She and her family were well-known tightrope walkers. Upside down tightrope walkers, it was true. Sarah was soon scuttling along the washing line. She gave the string a quick nibble and there were the nuts on the grass again!

Mum was annoyed! "I'll fix that squirrel," she said. So she replaced the string from which the box was hung with a piece of wire. "Let's

see her nibble through that," Mum said.

Well Sarah couldn't, of course. But she could still get at the box. It just meant that eating the nuts through the wire mesh was slow and a nuisance. But Sarah was not going to let things defeat her. She soon worked out how to pull out the peg that opened the lid at the bottom of the box so that all the nuts fell to the ground. The blue tits and the starlings in the garden were most impressed! That Sarah Squirrel is pretty clever, they thought.

"I am not going to allow a squirrel to beat me!" said Mum. So she thought and thought until she came up with a new idea. She took one of those large empty plastic lemonade bottles, cut the bottom out of it and then threaded it onto the wire on which the nut box hung. So now Sarah Squirrel would have to climb down that to get to the nut box. And Mum knew the bottle would be far too slippery for Sarah to get a grip.

So it was. Sarah tried of course, but she could not get a grip on the bottle and she fell off each time.

That was what had made Sarah so cross and her tail quivered with annoyance. However, she was not going to be beaten. She decided on something very daring. Or it would seem very daring to us, but to a squirrel it was just a little bit daring. For Sarah, like all her family, was a great leaper. The squirrels would often travel through the tree tops, leaping from branch to branch and from tree to tree. So why shouldn't Sarah just leap from the tree and land on the nut box?

She took a deep breath and worked out just how hard to jump and how far she needed to go. Then with a great bound she flew through the air and grabbed the nut box firmly as she landed on it. Next she got to work pulling out the peg to open the box and all the nuts fell to the ground!

The birds in the garden and the children who were watching were full of admiration.

"Look, Mum, look!" the children cried. "Look what the squirrel has done now. And doesn't she look sweet sitting up and holding a nut in her paws as she eats it? And wasn't she brave and clever to make such a jump?"

Mum agreed, "Oh well, perhaps I'll give up," she said. "I think that squirrel has beaten me. And after a jump like that she deserves a few nuts."

Sarah Squirrel chattered with

pleasure. "I've shown them," she thought, "you can't keep a good squirrel down!"

A Tale of Two Pigs

Dick King-Smith

"You told me that Fifi was a very wise cat," said Georgina to her grandfather, "but it seems to me that she says silly things sometimes. She told me that you once had a dog that fed a piglet. That can't be true."

"Oh, but it is," said her grandfather. "The dog was called Anna and she was a black-and-tan smooth-haired dachshund."

"What was the piglet called?" asked Georgina.

"It didn't have a name, but its mother was called Olwen and its aunt was called Blodwen."

"Do piglets have aunts?" said Georgina.

"Of course they do. Your mother's sister is your aunt, isn't she? And Olwen and Blodwen were sisters. They were Gloucester Old Spot pigs, and though they had their spots in different places, in every other way they were alike – sensible, friendly, quiet young sows. And they liked me to treat them exactly the same. They'd come to the front of the sty that they shared, and with one voice they'd say, 'Scratch my back.' And when I'd done that, they'd say, 'Hurry up, now. Fetch me my breakfast.'"

"Did they always do everything at the same time?" asked Georgina.

"They did," said her grandfather, "even to having their first litters of babies on the same day. Blodwen had hers in the early morning – seven of them, and Olwen had hers that evening."

"Seven too?"

"Of course," said her grandfather. "But that was the day when the likeness between them stopped."

"Why? What happened?"

"Blodwen – you could see straight away – was going to be a very good mother. 'Look!' she said when I came into her sty (she and Olwen had separate sties by now), 'Look! Aren't they beautiful! All big and healthy and all well-spotted. Did you ever see such lovely babies?' And she got to her feet ever so carefully so as not to tread on any, and let me see them while she had her breakfast, and then lay down again, ever so carefully so as not to squash any, and began to feed them. But Olwen wasn't like that.

"It sometimes happens with

animals, you know, when they have their first babies, that they can't understand what's happened and they don't feel a bit motherly and they won't have anything to do with their children. And that's what happened with Olwen.

'Ugh!' she shouted when the first one was born. 'Horrible wriggly little thing, whatever is it? Take it away!' And it was just the same when the rest of them arrived!"

"So what did you do?" asked Georgina.

"Luckily Blodwen had masses of milk, so I put them in with her lot and she settled down with all thirteen."

"Thirteen?" said Georgina. She did a sum on her fingers. "You said they had seven each, Grampa. That makes fourteen."

"You're right, clever clogs," said her grandfather. "But one of Olwen's seven was very small and weakly, so I took him into the house and put him in a basket in front of the fire, and that's where Anna the dachshund came in.

"She was very motherly, Anna was. She didn't have to have puppies of her own to come into milk. She'd do it at the sight of other puppies, or kittens, even. She came into the room now and looked at the little runt and said, 'Dear little thing,' just as I was saying, 'Poor little wretch.'

"Off I went to warm up some milk to bottle-feed the baby, but when I got back, Anna was suckling it!

'Take that bottle away,' she said (Anna was very bossy as well as very motherly). 'Cows' milk's not

good enough for this little chap.
You just leave him to me!'"

"So Fifi was right," said
Georgina. "You really did have a
dog that fed a piglet."

"Fifi was right," said her
grandfather. "As usual. Anna fed
that little runt till he was strong
enough to be put back."

"With his mother?"

"No, not with Olwen. I tried to make her accept her own babies, but she wouldn't.

'Don't you bring those horrible little things anywhere near me!' she snorted. 'I'm warning you!'

"But Blodwen managed to bring up all fourteen (and this time I *do* mean fourteen, because, thanks to Anna, the runt was strong enough to join his brothers and sisters and his cousins, and be fed by his kind Auntie Blodwen)."

Georgina sighed.

"I do like stories with happy endings," she said.

Sam, the Wee Fat Dog's Rotten Picnic

Ann McDonagh Bengtsson

Sam is a dog, a wee fat dog, who likes to take life

very

very

easy.

He lives with Jim in a bungalow on the edge of a little town somewhere in Scotland.

Sam likes to spend most of the

winter in front of Jim's fire, dreaming of sausages and juicy bones. With short legs and a fat tummy, he's just no good out in the rain or snow. On bad, squelchy days he goes . . . one two, splosh, shiver . . . three four. Brr, no fun at all!

In the summer, Sam loves to lie

under the big tree in the garden,
guarding his bone hole from the
cat who lives next door with Mrs
McGinty. Sometimes Jim takes
Sam for a walk and that's just
what happened one day last June.

When Jim got up, the sun was
shining fit to burst. "What a lovely
day," he thought. Then he had a
bright idea. "Why don't we have a
picnic? I'll go and waken Sam."

Sam, the wee fat dog, was still
fast asleep in his basket, snoring
his head off, dreaming about lots
of sausages laid out in a row. All
he had to do was walk along
eating them. Then he heard . . .
"Sam, Sam, Sam . . ."

He nearly jumped through the roof. "Oh no, a sausage is talking back. Maybe I shouldn't have eaten so many." But it wasn't a talking sausage. It was Jim.

"Come on, you lazy dog. We're going on a picnic."

"What's a picnic?" thought Sam. "Is it like a bus? Where do you go on it?"

Jim was too busy to explain. He got two plastic bags and began to put in everything they both liked best.

He packed sandwiches, cheesy crisps, an apple, a bar of chocolate and a can of fizzy orange for himself.

Sam sat drooling and dribbling, his tongue hanging out, when he saw what went into his bag.

"Oh, lovely . . . two sausages, doggy treats and a chocolate mouse. I'll just eat that stuff now, Jim." Sam pushed his nose into the bag.

"Oh, no you don't," cried Jim. "That's the whole idea. We take the grub with us and eat it in a field."

"That's daft," thought Sam, "but if it makes Jim happy, fine. I don't care where we eat it, as long as we eat it."

Jim put on his backpack. Off they went, down the road, past the post office, across the bridge and up the hill. Sam's tummy got emptier with every step and his wee stubby legs grew more and more tired by the minute.

"Jim, can't we stop soon?" he panted.

Jim cut across the field. "Nearly there, Sam. Isn't this lovely?"

"Lovely, my foot," growled Sam. "I want my grub . . ." Then an awful thing happened.

Just as they got to the top of the hill, puffing like engines, Sam saw a big rabbit. Sam likes rabbits because they look like cats with long ears and they run away . . . but they don't have nasty claws

186

and they don't spit.

"A rabbit!" yelped Sam. Off he ran as fast as he could, his wee legs going like mad and his tummy wobbling from side to side.

"Come back, you daft dog," shouted Jim. "You're not to chase rabbits. They're too fast for you. Sam! Sam!"

Sam didn't hear a word. He ran right on. And as I'm sure you've guessed already, the rabbit dashed down a hole.

Sam tried to get after it, but fat dogs don't fit in rabbit holes. Poor Sam was stuck.

The rabbit ran out of another hole and rolled about laughing.

187

Then the rest of his family came out of twenty more holes in the hill and they all rolled about laughing and making fun of poor wee Sam.

Sam's bahooky was stuck up in the air and his short back legs waved about.

"Get me out! Oh, Jim, save me, it's dark in here. They'll come and bite my nose!" he yelped.

Jim came puffing up and started to pull Sam's legs.

"Oh, my legs, my legs," yowled Sam.

Jim got a grip round his middle instead and gave a great big tug. There was a . . . sssch . . . schplopp, and Sam came flying out on top of Jim . . . who fell backwards right onto his backpack.

Their lovely grub was flattened and horrible. The sausages and the chocolate mouse got mixed up and the doggy treats were smashed to smithereens.

Sam could have cried. "I'll eat it anyway, Jim," he whined. "It will taste the same. I don't mind."

"We can't eat that stuff, Sam," said Jim in disgust. "Och, this is a rotten picnic. Come on, we're going home."

The pair of them slunk back, hungry and sad. Sam had his tail between his legs and he snuffled, "Whine and moan, we're going home," all the way.

Just as they reached the gate, feeling really sorry for themselves, out came Mrs McGinty from next door.

"What's the matter, you two? Have you dropped a pound and

found five pence?"

"We've had a rotten picnic, Mrs McGinty," explained Jim. "And I've nothing left to eat in the house."

Poor Sam put his paws over his eyes and howled blue murder.

"Oh, you poor wee dog," said Mrs McGinty. "Listen, Jim, you cleaned the snow off the path for me last winter, and Sam fetches my paper in the mornings, even if he does chew it a bit as well. I've just made a load of pies and a big apple cake. Would you like some? I can give you a pint of milk, too, if you want."

"Oh, yes please! Thanks very

much, Mrs McGinty." Jim was all smiles again.

Sam jumped up and licked any bit of her he could reach.

"You're a nice dog, Sam," she laughed, and went in to get the grub.

The sun was still shining, so they sat under the big tree on a rug from Jim's bed and ate the pies and the apple cake. Then they drank the milk.

"You know, Sam, this is the best place to have a picnic," said Jim.

"I could have told you that if you'd asked me, Jim." Sam wagged his tail and licked up the last drops of milk.

Papa Hedgehog and the Hare

Annette Elizabeth Clark

It had been a very wet day. The rain had poured steadily from the grey sky; the birds had stayed quiet in the trees and hedges; and all the little creatures of the woods and fields had kept snug in their holes and burrows. But towards evening the rain had stopped, the sky cleared, and the

sun shone out as if he was pleased
to see all the world looking so
bright and clean after the washing
the clouds had given it.

Papa Hedgehog came creeping
out of his hole (it was underneath
a thick blackthorn bush, just on
the edge of the wood). He looked
round him. "I think," he said to his
wife, "I shall take a little walk in
the cabbage field. It is a fine
evening and so fresh after the rain.
Really it is a pleasure to watch
those cabbages grow, so large and
handsome as they are and so cool
and shady when the sun is hot.
Besides," said Papa Hedgehog,
"one finds delightful company

there. The beetles are quite the pleasantest I have ever met."

(I am afraid the beetles were more pleasant to Papa Hedgehog than he was to the beetles. For to tell the truth, he liked them so much that he *ate* them! But that has nothing to do with this story.)

"Do go, my love," said Mamma Hedgehog. "I will follow you as soon as possible. As you say, it is a fine evening, and a walk will do you good."

So Papa Hedgehog trotted off on his four little legs, with his bright eyes and sharp nose, finding all kinds of good things to see and smell. The cabbages certainly were very handsome; their leaves were so broad and firm and green, and large, round, shining raindrops lay on them, sparkling like the clearest crystal. Papa Hedgehog sipped a little water from the hollow of a leaf and trotted on, keeping a sharp look-out for the beetles whose company he enjoyed so much.

Suddenly there was a scurry and a scuffle among the cabbages, and – almost on top of Papa Hedgehog – out bounced a large brown Hare, sending a shower of raindrops flying and upsetting quite a little pool of water from a big leaf over Papa Hedgehog's head and into his eyes and nose. Papa Hedgehog was startled, and he did as he always does when anything frightens him – he rolled himself into a tight little ball and stayed quite still for some minutes. Then he cautiously began to unroll, and the first thing his little bright eyes lit upon was the Hare sitting there laughing.

Papa Hedgehog sneezed and shook his head. He was a good-natured little fellow, and though the Hare had startled him he was not vexed. But if you or I had upset water all over a respectable old gentleman who was out for an evening walk we should at least say, "I am sorry."

The Hare did nothing of the kind. He laughed and laughed till he nearly fell over with laughing. "You can't think how funny you looked," he said. "You hedgehogs are funny anyhow, all just alike, with your round bodies and crooked legs. But I never saw you look so ridiculous as you did just

now. Oh, dear! Oh, dear! Oh, dear!"
said the Hare. And this time he
really did fall over sideways with
laughing.

"My legs are very good and
useful legs," said Papa Hedgehog
in a dignified voice, "and they are
much better than your *manners*,
which are very bad indeed. Good
evening," said Papa Hedgehog, and
he turned round to go home again,
for the Hare had quite upset him
and spoiled his evening walk.

But the Hare shouted "Crooked-
legs" so loudly after him that he
stopped. A thought came into his
little head, and he smiled to
himself. "The Hare says we are all

alike and all ridiculous, does he?
Well, he shall see. It is time he had
a lesson," said Papa Hedgehog.

So he came trotting back. "My
legs may be crooked," he said to
the Hare, "but that is no reason
why you should laugh at them. Let
us run a race and see who is the
winner. You may be very much
surprised!"

"A race indeed," said the Hare. "I
can run a mile while you creep a
yard."

"Try and see," said Papa
Hedgehog. "It is moonlight
tonight, and the next field has
been ploughed. I will run up one
furrow. You shall run up the next.

When you get to the end you shall see!"

"Very well, old Crooked-legs," said the rude Hare. "I'll be there, waiting to laugh at you." And away he went with a hop, skip and jump of his long legs, over the bank, through the hedge, and across the fields, while Papa Hedgehog trotted home to his wife.

"My love," said he, "we are to play a little game with the Hare tonight," and he told Mamma Hedgehog his plan; and they both chuckled so much that they rolled themselves into tight balls with laughing.

Presently – just a little while

before the moon rose – Mamma Hedgehog trotted out and away into the dark. Papa Hedgehog had told her where to go and what to do, and by-and-by, when the moon was up, he followed. Past the cabbage field, where the cabbages looked as if they were made of ivory and silver in the moonlight, he scuttled – through the hedge – and there lay the ploughed field with its long, deep, dark furrows. A minute or two later the Hare came running swiftly along the edge of the field.

"Hullo, old Crooked-legs," he said, "are you ready to start?"

"Yes," said Papa Hedgehog. "I am

quite ready. I will take the furrow nearest the hedge. You take the next. Are you ready? *Off!*"

Away went the Hare, bounding easily up the furrow. He did not hurry very much; he thought there was no need. "Poor fellow," he said scornfully to himself, "his crooked legs must be working very hard to carry that fat little round body. Probably he will die for want of breath before he is halfway up the furrow. Well, it is not my fault," said the Hare. And with one long jump he reached the end of the course.

But just as he got there, a little head with two bright eyes and a sharp nose peeped out of the next furrow, and a little voice said, "Here I am, you see!" It was Mamma Hedgehog who was waiting for him; but the Hare did not know that. One hedgehog looked just like another to him, especially by moonlight, and he thought Papa Hedgehog had got there first! His big eyes nearly popped out of his head with surprise. He did not wait one minute to think.

"I'll beat you next time," he said in a great hurry; and he turned round and flew down the furrow, leaving Mamma Hedgehog chuckling behind him.

"Fancy old Crooked-legs running so fast," said the Hare to himself as he ran, "but he can never keep it up. He is probably dead by now!"

But when he was nearly at the end of the course a little head with a sharp nose and two bright eyes peeped out of the next furrow, and a little voice said, "Here I am, you see!" It was Papa Hedgehog, who had been sitting there very comfortably, waiting for him.

"*You*!" said the Hare, very much out of breath.

"Yes, *me*," said Papa Hedgehog.

"I'll beat you next time," said the Hare, and he raced up the furrow again.

But Mamma Hedgehog was ready for him, and back went the Hare once more. Up and down he raced, up and down. The time went by, and the full moon came sailing higher and higher up the sky. It seemed as if there was a broad smile on its face at the sight of the Hare running so fast along the furrow, while Papa and Mamma Hedgehog waited for him, one at each end.

Up and down he went, up and down; he was all out of breath, he was giddy and panting and puzzled. It was really a terrible race! And at last he was so tired he really could run no more; right in

the middle of the furrow he
tumbled down and went to sleep,
and never woke up till sunrise
next morning. And Papa and
Mamma Hedgehog trotted off
chuckling, to find their supper,
and then they went home to sleep.

As for the Hare, next time he saw

Papa Hedgehog coming, he went a long way round to avoid meeting him. He was afraid Papa Hedgehog would laugh!

How the tale of the race came to be told I do not know; Papa and Mamma Hedgehog are quiet folk and do not talk much, and certainly the Hare never spoke of it. Perhaps it was the Man in the Moon! But whoever told it first, it has certainly been told a great many times since, and now I'm telling it again for you.

The Butterfly Who Sang

Terry Jones

A butterfly was once sitting on a leaf looking extremely sad.

"What's wrong?" asked a friendly frog.

"Oh," said the butterfly, "nobody really appreciates me," and she parted her beautiful red and blue wings and shut them again.

"What d'you mean?" asked the frog. "I've seen you flying about and thought to myself: that is one beautiful butterfly! All my friends think you look great, too! You're a real stunner!"

"Oh *that*," replied the butterfly, and she opened her wings again. "Who cares about *looks*? It's my singing that nobody appreciates."

"I've never heard your singing; but if it's anywhere near as good as your looks, you've got it made!" said the frog.

"That's the trouble," replied the butterfly, "people say they can't hear my singing. I suppose it's so refined and so high that their ears aren't sensitive enough to pick it up."

"But I bet it's great all the

same!" said the frog.

"It is," said the butterfly. "Would you like me to sing for you?"

"Well . . . I don't suppose my ears are sensitive enough to pick it up, but I'll give it a try!" said the frog.

So the butterfly spread her wings, and opened her mouth. The frog gazed in wonder at the butterfly's beautiful wings, for he'd never been so close to them before.

The butterfly sang on and on, and still the frog gazed at her wings, absolutely captivated, even though he could hear nothing whatsoever of her singing.

Eventually, however, the butterfly stopped, and closed up

her wings.

"Beautiful!" said the frog, thinking about the wings.

"Thank you," said the butterfly, thrilled that at last she had found an appreciative listener.

After that, the frog came every day to listen to the butterfly sing, though all the time he was really feasting his eyes on her beautiful wings. And every day, the butterfly tried harder and harder to impress the frog with her singing, even though he could not hear a note of it. But one day a moth, who was jealous of all the attention the butterfly was getting, took the butterfly on one side and said,

"Butterfly, your singing is quite superb."

"Thank you," said the butterfly.

"With just a little more practise," said the cunning moth, "you could be as famous a singer as the nightingale."

"Do you think so?" asked the butterfly, flattered beyond words.

"I certainly do," replied the moth. "Indeed, perhaps you already *do* sing better than the nightingale, only it's difficult to concentrate on your music because your gaudy wings are so distracting."

"Is that right?" said the butterfly.

"I'm afraid so," said the moth.

"You notice the nightingale is wiser, and wears only dull brown feathers so as not to distract from her singing."

"You're right!" cried the butterfly. "I was a fool not to have realised that before!" And straight away she found some earth and rubbed it into her wings until they were all grey and half the colours had rubbed off.

The next day, the frog arrived for the concert as usual, but when the butterfly opened her wings he cried out, "Oh! Butterfly! What have you done to your beautiful wings?" And the butterfly explained what she had done.

"I think you will find," she said, "that now you will be able to concentrate more on my music."

Well, the poor frog tried, but it was no good, for of course he couldn't hear anything at all. So he soon became bored, and hopped off into the pond. And after that the butterfly never *could* find anyone to listen to her singing.

ACKNOWLEDGEMENTS

The publishers wish to thank the following for permission to reproduce copyright material:

Joyce Lankester Brisley: "Milly-Molly-Mandy Minds a Baby" from *Further Doings of Milly-Molly-Mandy* by Joyce Lankester Brisley; first published by Harrap 1932 and reproduced by permission of Chambers Harrap Publishers Ltd.

Ann McDonagh Bengtsson: "Sam, the Wee Fat Dog's Rotten Picnic" from *Sam, the Wee Fat Dog* by Ann McDonagh Bengtsson; first published by Corgi, a division of Transworld Publishers 1996, pp. 5–31 and reproduced with their permission. Copyright © Ann McDonagh Bengtsson.

John Cotton: "Sarah Squirrel's Triumph"; reproduced by permission of the author.

Ann Cameron: "Tracks" from *The Stories Huey Tells* by Ann Cameron; first published by Victor Gollancz/Hamish Hamilton 1995, pp. 57–70. Copyright © Ann Cameron 1995. Reproduced by permission of Hamish Hamilton Ltd and Alfred A. Knopf, a division of Random House, Inc.

Margaret Mahy: "The Runaway Reptiles" from *Bubble Trouble* by Margaret Mahy; first published by Hamish Hamilton 1991 and reproduced by permission of Vanessa Hamilton Books Ltd.

Carolyn Haywood: "Eddie and the Goat" from *Eddie and the Fire Engine* by Carolyn Haywood; first published by HarperCollins Publishers, Inc. and reproduced with their permission. Copyright © 1949 by Carolyn Haywood.

Elizabeth Clark: "Papa Hedgehog and the Hare" from *Country Tales* by Elizabeth Clark; first published by Hodder and Stoughton 1996, pp. 13–21 and reproduced with their permission.

Sheila Lavelle: "When You Are Six" from *Round About Six (Stories and Poems chosen by Kaye Webb)*; first published by Frances Lincoln 1992, pp. 62–9 and reproduced by permission of Sheila Lavelle.

Andrew Matthews: "Fox's Revenge" from *The Beasts of Boggart Hollow* by Andrew Matthews; first published by The Orion Publishing Group Ltd in 1996, pp. 68–75 and reproduced with their permission.

Terry Jones: "The Butterfly Who Sang" from *Fairy Tales* by Terry Jones; first published by Pavilion Books 1981 and reproduced with their permission.

ACKNOWLEDGEMENTS

Anita Hewitt: "Elephant Big and Elephant Little" from *The Anita Hewitt Animal Story* by Anita Hewitt; first published by Red Fox 1972 and reproduced by permission of Random House UK.

Dorothy Edwards: "The Dog Who Frightened the Sea" from *The Old Man Who Sneezed* by Dorothy Edwards; first published by Methuen Children's Books 1983, pp. 54–60. Copyright © Dorothy Edwards 1983. Reproduced by permission of Rogers, Coleridge and White Ltd.

Dick King-Smith: " One Very Small Foot" from *Sophie' Snail* by Dick King-Smith, first published in 1988, and "A Tale of Two Pigs" from *Farm Tales* by Dick King-Smith, first published in 1992, pp. 19–23. Reproduced by permission of A. P. Watt Ltd on behalf of Fox Busters Ltd.

Mary Rayner: "Mr and Mrs Pig's Evening Out" from *Mr and Mrs Pig's Evening Out* by Mary Rayner; first published by Macmillan Children's Books and reproduced by permission of the author.

Every effort has been made to trace the copyright holders but if any have been inadvertently overlooked the publishers will be pleased to make the necessary arrangement at the first opportunity.